This story belongs to:

_____

The Forever Journal

A LIFETIME OF MEMORIES

A Keepsake Journal and Memory Book to Capture Your Life Story

Ashley Sirah Nicole Chea

Clarkson Potter/Publishers
New York

CONTENTS

Let your memories tell stories for the future.

INTRODUCTION

History is a gift. It allows us to understand where we came from and discover who we can become. We can learn so much from how our parents and grandparents grew up—from how they were raised to the paths they chose—and gain insight into the experiences that shaped their lives. Now that I'm an adult, I realize how much of a role my childhood played in shaping the person I am, and, as a mother, I hope to pass on what I have learned through my experiences to my children.

My sister tragically died when she was twenty-four years old, leaving behind her three-year-old son. As he grew up, he became increasingly curious about the mother he never truly got to know. Of course, I shared her stories to the best of my ability, but I'm constantly reminded that he will never get to hear them in his mother's own words.

Once I went to therapy, did a lot of healing, and became a mother myself, I realized how important it is for us to tell our own stories. This journal is your chance to do just that—to share your thoughts, advice, and memories, and allow your family to get to know you for the unique and beautiful human you are. Our experiences enable people to connect with and learn from us while we're here and after we're gone. I hope you find peace, healing, and love while sharing your story.

—Ashley Sirah Nicole Chea

PART ONE

Growing Up

paste photo here

My full name:

_____

How my parents chose my name:

_____

_____

_____

_____

_____

My nickname(s) growing up and why:

_____

_____

_____

_____

My birthday: _____ Time of birth: _____

Where I was born: _____

_____

My parents' names:

_____

_____

_____

My parents' birthdays:

_____

_____

_____

My parents' jobs:

_____

_____

_____

_____

_____

How I would describe my parents:

_____

_____

_____

_____

_____

_____

_____

_____

_____

Personality traits and characteristics that I inherited from my parents:

_____

_____

_____

_____

_____

My grandparents' names:

_____

_____

_____

_____

My grandparents' jobs:

_____

_____

_____

_____

How I would describe my grandparents:

_____

_____

_____

_____

_____

_____

_____

What I learned from my parents, grandparents, and/or caregivers:

_____

_____

_____

_____

_____

_____

_____

_____

_____

_____

_____

_____

_____

_____

_____

My siblings' names:

_____

_____

_____

_____

_____

My relationship with my siblings growing up:

_____

_____

_____

_____

_____

_____

_____

_____

_____

_____

My relationship with my siblings now:

_____

_____

_____

_____

_____

_____

_____

_____

_____

_____

_____

_____

_____

_____

_____

_____

THE FOREVER JOURNAL

2nd great-grandparents   great-grandparents   grandparents   parent

parent   grandparents   great-grandparents   2nd great-grandparents

My childhood pet(s), and their name(s):

_____

_____

_____

_____

Activities my family enjoyed doing together:

_____

_____

_____

_____

_____

_____

_____

_____

_____

_____

_____

_____

Places my family lived:

_____

_____

_____

_____

_____

_____

How I would describe my childhood home(s):

_____

_____

_____

_____

_____

_____

_____

_____

_____

My religion growing up:

_____

How I identify now in terms of religion:

_____

_____

_____

My favorite childhood memories:

_____

_____

_____

_____

_____

_____

_____

_____

_____

My favorite age and why:

_____

_____

_____

_____

_____

_____

_____

What I wanted to be when I grew up:

_____

_____

_____

_____

_____

_____

_____

My favorite place(s) as a child:

_____

_____

_____

_____

_____

_____

_____

_____

_____

_____

_____

_____

_____

_____

_____

My favorite TV shows, movies, music, and books growing up:

_____

_____

_____

_____

_____

_____

_____

My favorite childhood toy(s):

_____

_____

_____

_____

_____

_____

_____

_____

My favorite childhood activities:

_____

_____

_____

_____

_____

_____

_____

My childhood best friends:

_____

_____

_____

_____

_____

_____

_____

What I miss most about being a child:

_____

_____

_____

_____

_____

_____

_____

The biggest lesson(s) I learned in my childhood:

_____

_____

_____

_____

_____

_____

_____

What I wish I could tell my ten-year-old self:

_____

_____

_____

_____

_____

What I wish I could tell my sixteen-year-old self:

_____

_____

_____

_____

_____

What I wish I could tell my twenty-one-year-old self:

_____

_____

_____

_____

_____

What my life was like when I was growing up, in my own words:

_____

_____

_____

_____

_____

_____

_____

_____

_____

_____

_____

_____

_____

_____

_____

_____

_____

PART TWO

Parenthood

Your birthday(s):

_____

_____

_____

_____

_____

Your time(s) of birth:

_____

_____

_____

_____

_____

Your birth weight(s):

_____

_____

_____

_____

Your length(s) at birth:

_____

_____

_____

_____

Where you were born:

_____

_____

_____

_____

_____

My memories from the day you were born:

_____

_____

_____

_____

_____

_____

_____

_____

_____

_____

_____

_____

_____

_____

How your name(s) was/were chosen:

_____

_____

_____

_____

_____

_____

Your nickname(s) growing up and why:

_____

_____

_____

_____

Your first word(s):

_____

_____

_____

_____

What I thought I knew about parenthood when I first became a parent:

_____

_____

_____

_____

_____

_____

_____

What I know now about parenthood:

_____

_____

_____

_____

_____

_____

_____

Why I decided to become a parent:

_____

_____

_____

_____

_____

_____

_____

How I felt when I was awaiting your arrival:

_____

_____

_____

_____

_____

_____

_____

My support system when I had you:

_____

_____

_____

_____

_____

_____

_____

As a new parent, I felt these emotions:

_____

_____

_____

_____

_____

_____

_____

Unexpected joys of parenthood:

_____

_____

_____

_____

_____

_____

_____

Unexpected challenges of parenthood:

_____

_____

_____

_____

_____

_____

_____

How my life changed when you were born:

_____

_____

_____

_____

_____

_____

_____

How I practiced self-care when you were born:

_____

_____

_____

_____

_____

_____

_____

My funniest memory from your childhood:

_____

_____

_____

_____

_____

_____

_____

My favorite memories from your childhood:

_____

_____

_____

_____

_____

_____

_____

How I would describe you as a child:

_____

_____

_____

_____

_____

_____

_____

_____

The personality traits and characteristics you inherited from me:

_____

_____

_____

_____

_____

_____

_____

_____

The personality traits and characteristics you inherited from your other parent:

_____

_____

_____

_____

_____

_____

_____

I was surprised when you _____ :

_____

_____

_____

_____

_____

_____

_____

Your favorite toy(s) as a child:

_____

_____

_____

_____

_____

Your favorite activities as a child:

_____

_____

_____

_____

_____

Favorite family vacations:

_____

_____

_____

_____

_____

Favorite family traditions:

_____

_____

_____

_____

_____

_____

_____

Our favorite thing to do as a family when you were growing up:

_____

_____

_____

_____

_____

_____

_____

Don't look
to be who you
were before
you had a baby.
Embrace the
new version
of yourself.

Here are some ways I discovered and embraced the "new" me:

_____

_____

_____

_____

_____

_____

_____

_____

_____

_____

_____

_____

_____

_____

_____

_____

_____

What I learned about myself when trying to parent
with my spouse, partner, or alone:

_____

_____

_____

_____

_____

_____

How I would describe my parenting style:

_____

_____

_____

_____

_____

_____

Why I chose my parenting style:

_____

_____

_____

_____

_____

_____

_____

If I could do it over, what I would or would not change
about how I disciplined you:

_____

_____

_____

_____

_____

_____

_____

_____

My proudest moments as a parent:

My greatest strengths as a parent:

_____

_____

_____

_____

_____

_____

_____

My weaknesses as a parent:

_____

_____

_____

_____

_____

_____

_____

The lessons I've learned from parenthood:

_____

_____

_____

_____

_____

_____

_____

_____

_____

_____

_____

_____

_____

_____

_____

_____

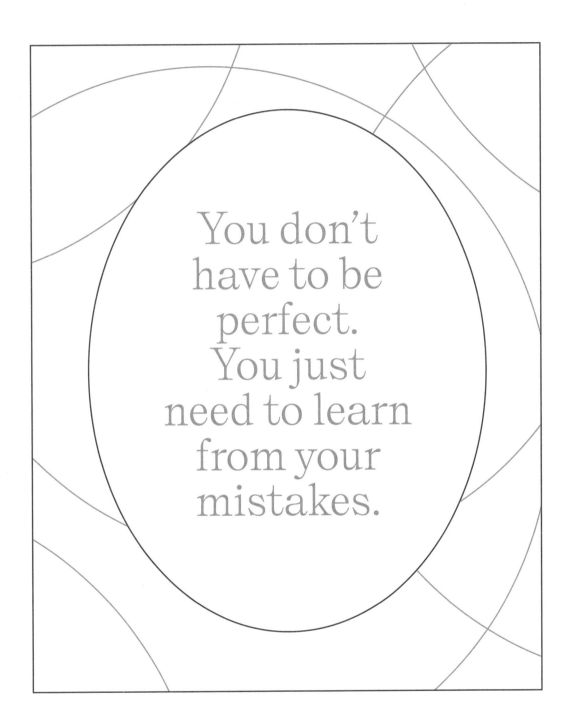

You don't have to be perfect. You just need to learn from your mistakes.

What I'm most grateful for about parenthood:

_____

_____

_____

_____

_____

_____

_____

If I could do it all over again as a parent, here's what I would change:

_____

_____

_____

_____

_____

_____

_____

My favorite parenting advice:

_____

_____

_____

_____

_____

_____

_____

_____

_____

_____

_____

_____

_____

_____

_____

PART THREE

Love and Friendship

What my first love was like:

_____

_____

_____

_____

_____

_____

_____

What my first love would say about me:

_____

_____

_____

_____

_____

_____

_____

What I learned from my first love and how that has affected how I love now:

_____

_____

_____

_____

_____

_____

_____

_____

_____

_____

_____

_____

_____

_____

_____

_____

_____

What I thought I knew about love when I was younger:

_____

_____

_____

_____

_____

_____

_____

What love means to me now:

_____

_____

_____

_____

_____

_____

_____

How to know when you're in love:

_____

_____

_____

_____

_____

_____

_____

_____

_____

_____

_____

_____

_____

_____

_____

_____

What I want you to know about romantic relationships:

_____

_____

_____

_____

_____

_____

_____

_____

_____

_____

_____

_____

_____

_____

_____

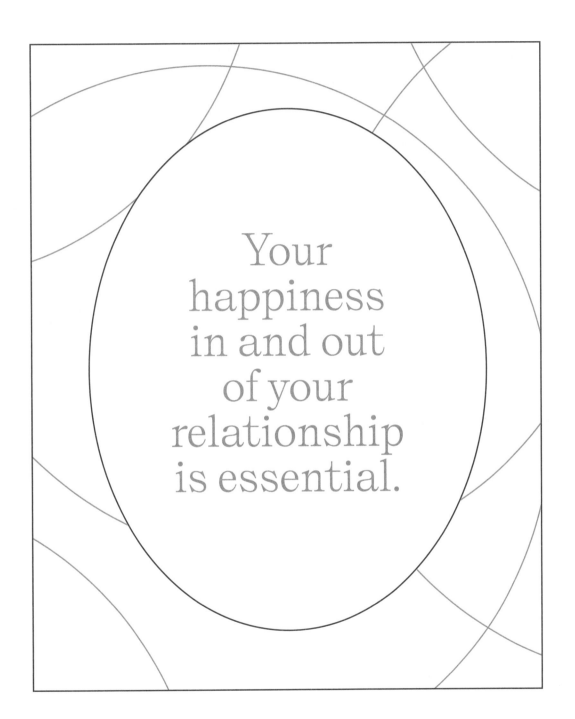

Your
happiness
in and out
of your
relationship
is essential.

How to maintain your independence when you're
in a committed relationship:

_____

_____

_____

_____

_____

_____

_____

_____

_____

_____

_____

_____

_____

_____

_____

The greatest lesson I learned about love:

_____

_____

_____

_____

_____

_____

_____

_____

_____

_____

_____

_____

_____

_____

How I met your other parent:

_____

_____

_____

_____

_____

_____

_____

_____

_____

_____

_____

_____

_____

_____

_____

_____

Why I fell for your other parent:

_____

_____

_____

_____

_____

_____

_____

Why I decided to or not to get married:

_____

_____

_____

_____

_____

_____

_____

_____

Our engagement story:

_____

_____

_____

_____

_____

_____

_____

_____

_____

_____

_____

_____

_____

_____

My favorite part of my wedding day:

_____

_____

_____

_____

_____

_____

_____

_____

_____

_____

_____

_____

_____

_____

If you decide to get married, here's what I want you
to know on your wedding day:

_____

_____

_____

_____

_____

_____

_____

_____

_____

_____

_____

_____

_____

The joys of marriage/long-term relationships:

_____

_____

_____

_____

_____

_____

_____

The challenges of marriage/long-term relationships:

_____

_____

_____

_____

_____

_____

_____

What to remember when you and your partner
or spouse have conflicts or disagreements:

_____

_____

_____

_____

_____

_____

_____

_____

_____

_____

_____

_____

_____

_____

_____

If someone makes you feel like you don't matter, remember this:

_____

_____

_____

_____

_____

_____

_____

If you ever feel unsafe in your relationship, remember this:

_____

_____

_____

_____

_____

_____

_____

My biggest heartbreak and how I coped with it::

_____

_____

_____

_____

_____

_____

_____

_____

_____

_____

_____

_____

_____

_____

How to heal from heartbreak:

_____

_____

_____

_____

_____

_____

_____

_____

_____

_____

_____

_____

_____

_____

_____

_____

_____

_____

_____

If you ever decide you no longer want to be married or in a
committed relationship, ask yourself these questions:

_____

_____

_____

_____

_____

_____

_____

_____

_____

_____

_____

_____

_____

_____

_____

My best friends:

_____

_____

_____

_____

_____

What I learned about love through my friendships:

_____

_____

_____

_____

_____

_____

_____

_____

_____

How my best friend would describe the kind of friend I am:

_____

_____

_____

_____

_____

_____

_____

How I would describe the kind of friend I am:

_____

_____

_____

_____

_____

_____

_____

How to be a good friend:

_____

_____

_____

_____

_____

_____

_____

How to cope with losing friends:

_____

_____

_____

_____

_____

_____

_____

The greatest lesson I have learned about friendship:

_____

_____

_____

_____

_____

_____

_____

_____

_____

_____

_____

_____

_____

_____

_____

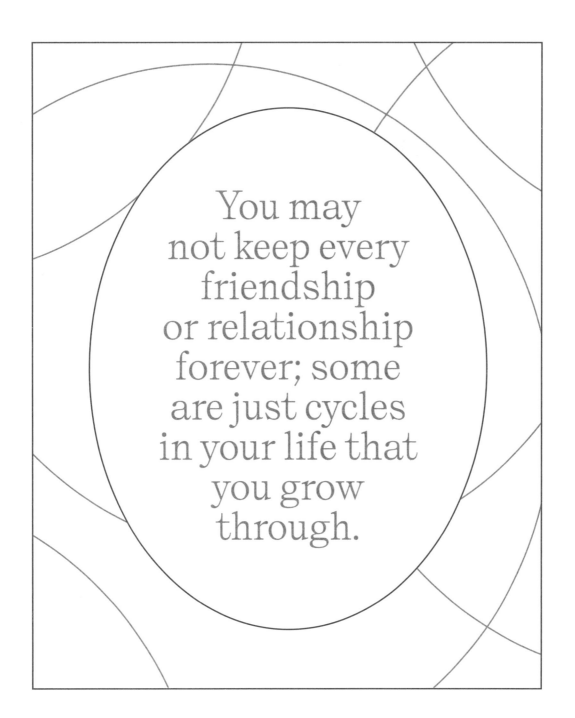

You may
not keep every
friendship
or relationship
forever; some
are just cycles
in your life that
you grow
through.

PART FOUR

Education
and Career

My high school:

_____

My favorite subject in high school and why:

_____

_____

_____

_____

_____

_____

Activities, clubs, or sports teams I was a part of in high school:

_____

_____

_____

_____

_____

_____

My favorite part of my high school experience:

_____

_____

_____

_____

_____

_____

My least favorite part of my high school experience:

_____

_____

_____

_____

A funny story about high school:

_____

_____

_____

_____

My college:

_____

My major and minor in college:

_____

_____

Why I chose my major and minor:

_____

_____

_____

_____

_____

Why I did or didn't go to college:

_____

_____

_____

_____

_____

Activities, clubs, or sports teams I was a part of in college:

_____

_____

_____

_____

_____

My favorite part of my college experience:

_____

_____

_____

_____

_____

My least favorite part of my college experience:

_____

_____

_____

_____

_____

A funny story about my college experience:

_____

_____

_____

_____

_____

My advice for choosing a college, if you decide to go:

_____

_____

_____

_____

_____

_____

_____

_____

_____

What I did instead of going to college:

_____

_____

_____

_____

_____

_____

The biggest lesson I learned from choosing a different
path than going to college:

_____

_____

_____

_____

_____

_____

_____

My career path:

_____

_____

_____

_____

_____

_____

_____

_____

_____

_____

_____

_____

_____

_____

_____

_____

Why and how I chose my career:

_____

_____

_____

_____

_____

_____

_____

What I hope you get out of your career path:

_____

_____

_____

_____

_____

_____

_____

It's okay
to start over.
You are never
too old to follow
a dream or
start a new
career.

How I made it to my dream job:

_____

_____

_____

_____

_____

_____

How my dream career has changed over the years:

_____

_____

_____

_____

_____

_____

_____

_____

_____

Why it is important to follow your dreams:

_____

_____

_____

_____

_____

_____

_____

_____

What prevented me from accomplishing my dreams:

_____

_____

_____

_____

_____

_____

_____

_____

Roadblocks I had to overcome in my career path:

_____

_____

_____

_____

_____

_____

_____

The most important things I learned about myself throughout my career:

_____

_____

_____

_____

_____

_____

_____

How to deal with people who don't believe in you:

_____

_____

_____

_____

_____

_____

_____

How to deal with imposter syndrome or feeling like you're
not "good enough" to be in a certain position:

_____

_____

_____

_____

_____

_____

_____

_____

How to cope with failure:

_____

_____

_____

_____

_____

_____

_____

_____

_____

_____

_____

_____

_____

_____

_____

_____

_____

_____

When I first started to make money and what I spent it on:

_____

_____

_____

_____

_____

_____

_____

_____

My best financial advice:

_____

_____

_____

_____

_____

_____

_____

_____

The greatest lessons I've learned throughout my education and career:

_____

_____

_____

_____

_____

_____

_____

_____

_____

_____

_____

_____

_____

_____

_____

_____

_____

_____

_____

_____

PART FIVE

Health
and Wellness

My daily health and wellness rituals:

_____
_____
_____
_____
_____
_____
_____

What I prioritize about my physical health:

_____
_____
_____
_____
_____
_____
_____

What I prioritize about my mental health:

_____

_____

_____

_____

_____

_____

_____

Why it's important to practice self-care:

_____

_____

_____

_____

_____

_____

_____

What self-care has looked like for me throughout my life:

_____

_____

_____

_____

_____

_____

_____

How I deal with dark days:

_____

_____

_____

_____

_____

_____

_____

Our family's health history:

_____

_____

_____

_____

_____

_____

_____

_____

_____

_____

_____

_____

_____

_____

_____

_____

PART SIX

Who I Am

My favorite movie(s):

_____

_____

_____

_____

_____

My favorite television show(s):

_____

_____

_____

_____

_____

My favorite food(s):

_____

_____

_____

_____

_____

My favorite recipe(s):

_____

_____

_____

_____

_____

_____

_____

_____

_____

_____

_____

_____

_____

_____

_____

_____

My favorite color(s):

_____

_____

My favorite book(s)

_____

_____

_____

_____

My favorite poem(s)

_____

_____

_____

_____

My favorite song(s):

_____

_____

_____

_____

My favorite quote(s):

_____

_____

_____

_____

_____

_____

_____

_____

_____

_____

_____

_____

_____

_____

_____

_____

My favorite place(s) to travel:

_____

_____

_____

_____

_____

The wildest thing I've ever done:

_____

_____

_____

_____

_____

_____

_____

_____

_____

My role models and the best lessons I've learned from them:

_____

_____

_____

_____

_____

_____

_____

_____

_____

_____

_____

_____

_____

_____

_____

The best thing that's ever happened to me:

_____
_____
_____
_____
_____
_____
_____

The worst thing that's ever happened to me:

_____
_____
_____
_____
_____
_____
_____

The best advice I've ever received:

_____

_____

_____

_____

_____

_____

_____

The best advice I've ever given:

_____

_____

_____

_____

_____

_____

_____

Roadblocks I had to overcome to get where I am today:

_____

_____

_____

_____

_____

_____

_____

_____

_____

_____

_____

_____

_____

_____

_____

_____

_____

One thing I would do differently if given the chance:

_____

_____

_____

_____

_____

_____

_____

_____

_____

_____

_____

_____

_____

_____

_____

What I did/am doing to live my most fulfilling life:

_____

_____

_____

_____

_____

One rule I live by:

_____

_____

_____

My biggest regret:

_____

_____

_____

_____

_____

_____

My greatest fear:

_____

_____

_____

_____

_____

_____

How I dealt with my fears and regrets:

_____

_____

_____

_____

_____

_____

_____

_____

_____

_____

_____

_____

WHO I AM

My best-kept secret:

_____

_____

_____

_____

Historic events that occurred during my lifetime:

_____

_____

_____

_____

_____

_____

_____

_____

_____

_____

How I want to be remembered:

_____

_____

_____

_____

_____

_____

_____

_____

_____

_____

_____

_____

_____

_____

_____

_____

My best life advice:

_____

_____

_____

_____

_____

_____

_____

_____

_____

_____

_____

_____

_____

_____

_____

_____

_____

PART SEVEN

My Story, in My Own Words

Published in the United States by Clarkson Potter/Publishers, an imprint of the
Crown Publishing Group, a division of Penguin Random House LLC, New York.
ClarksonPotter.com

CLARKSON POTTER is a trademark and POTTER with colophon
is a registered trademark of Penguin Random House LLC.

ISBN 978-0-593-58053-0

Printed in China

Editor: Sahara Clement
Designer: Lise Sukhu and Danielle Deschenes
Art Director: Danielle Deschenes
Production editor: Bridget Sweet
Production manager: Luisa Francavilla
Copyeditor: Diana Drew
Marketer: Chloe Aryeh

10 9 8 7 6 5 4 3 2 1

First Edition